W9-AUF-558

American Lives

Molly
Pitcher

Rick Burke

Heinemann Library
Chicago, Illinois

© 2003 Heinemann Library
a division of Reed Elsevier Inc.
Chicago, Illinois

Customer Service 888-454-2279

Visit our website at www.heinemannlibrary.com

Created by the publishing team
at Heinemann Library

Designed by Sarah Figlio
Photo Research by Dawn Friedman
Printed and Bound in the United States by
Lake Book Manufacturing, Inc.

07 06 05 04 03
10 9 8 7 6 5 4 3 2 1

Acknowledgments
The author and publishers are grateful to the
following for permission to reproduce copyright
material: Title page, pp. 5, 17 Bettmann/Corbis;
pp. 4, 7, 8, 13, 14, 18, 19, 20 North Wind Picture
Archives; pp. 9, 16, 21 Hulton Archive/Getty
Images; pp. 10, 12, 25, 28 Cumberland County
Historical Society, Carlisle, PA; p. 15 National
Portrait Gallery, Smithsonian Institution/Art
Resource; p. 22 Carl & Ann Purcell/Corbis; p. 23
The Granger Collection; p. 24 Courtesy of U.S.
Field Artillery Association; p. 26 West Point
Museum Art Collection, United States Military
Academy; p. 27 U.S. Military Academy Archives; p.
29 Les Stone/Sygma/Corbis

Cover photograph: Bettmann/Corbis

Special thanks to Patrick Halladay for his help in
the preparation of this book.

Every effort has been made to contact copyright
holders of any material reproduced in this book.
Any omissions will be rectified in subsequent
printings if notice is given to the publisher.

Library of Congress Cataloging-in-Publication Data
Burke, Rick, 1957-
  Molly Pitcher / Rick Burke.
     v. cm. — (American lives)
Includes bibliographical references and index.
Contents: Fire the cannon! — A future hero's family — Working on the farm —
Moving away — Carlisle and Marriage — War breaks out — Women and the war —
Valley Forge — Battle of Monmouth — Sergeant Molly — Molly's last years —
The other Molly Pitcher — Remembering the women of the war.
  ISBN 1-40340-727-4 (Library Binding-hardcover) — ISBN 1-40343-102-7 (Paperback)
  1. Pitcher, Molly, 1754-1832—Juvenile literature. 2. Monmouth, Battle of, Freehold, N.J., 1778—Juvenile
literature. 3. Corbin, Margaret Cochran, 1751-ca. 1800—Juvenile literature. 4. Women revolutionaries—
United States—Biography—Juvenile literature. 5. United States—History—Revolution, 1775-1783—
Women—Juvenile literature. 6. United States—History—Revolution, 1775-1783—Biography—Juvenile
literature. [1. Pitcher, Molly, 1754-1832. 2. Monmouth, Battle of, Freehold, N.J., 1778. 3. United States—
History—Revolution, 1775-1783 v Biography. 4. Women—Biography.] I. Title.
  E241.M7 B87 2003
  973.3'082—dc21
                                    2002154415

Some words are shown in bold, **like this.** You can
find out what they mean by looking in the glossary.

The cover of this book shows a portrait of Molly Pitcher at
the Battle of Monmouth on June 28, 1778.

Contents

Fire the Cannon!

Molly Pitcher could see smoke rising from the rifles and **cannons** of both armies on a battlefield of the **Revolutionary War.** The red-coated British soldiers were attacking the army of the newly formed United States, which was led by General George Washington.

Molly ran back and forth, carrying a pitcher of cold water. The water was for the thirsty, American soldiers. "Molly! Molly! I need water! Please bring me water!" Molly kept hearing the cries of the hot, tired soldiers.

Many drawings and paintings have been made to show what Molly Pitcher might have looked like. She is shown lighting a cannon in this drawing.

Molly Pitcher's husband had become overheated in the battle. He is shown lying by the side of the cannon in this painting.

Molly got the nickname Molly Pitcher because she carried water in a pitcher to American soldiers on the battlefield. Her real name was Mary Hays. She got the water from a well that was nearby.

Molly had a special reason for being on the battlefield on that hot June day in 1778. Her husband, William, was one of the American soldiers fighting the British. By carrying water, Molly was helping her husband fight for the freedom of all Americans. She ran to her husband's cannon to give him water. But when she got there, she saw him lying on the ground. Molly decided to help fire the cannon!

A Future Hero's Family

The woman who would later be called Molly Pitcher was born with the name Mary Ludwig. She was born on October 13, 1754. Her parents were John and Gretchen Ludwig.

John was born in the country of Germany, and Gretchen was from Holland. John and Gretchen came to the British **colonies** of America because they hoped their lives would be better than they were in Europe.

American Colonies

Lake Huron
Lake Ontario
Lake Erie
NEW YORK
MAINE (Part of Massachusetts)
NEW HAMPSHIRE
MASSACHUSETTS
RHODE ISLAND
CONNECTICUT
PENNSYLVANIA
Trenton
New York City
NEW JERSEY
DELAWARE
MARYLAND
VIRGINIA
ATLANTIC OCEAN
NORTH CAROLINA
SOUTH CAROLINA
GEORGIA

N
W E
S

| 0 | 250 miles |
| 0 | 400 kilometers |

Trenton, New Jersey, the town near where Mary grew up, is shown on this map.

The Life of Molly Pitcher

1754	1767	1769	1776
Born on October 13 near Trenton, New Jersey.	*Moved to Carlisle, Pennsylvania.*	*Married William Hays on July 24.*	*Followed husb to fight in* **Revolutionar** *War.*

John and Gretchen met soon after they arrived in the colonies and got married. They bought some land near Trenton, New Jersey, and started a dairy farm. The milk from the cows on the farm was sold or made into butter, cream, or cheese.

The dairy farm that Mary helped her parents run probably looked a lot like the farm in the painting above.

John and Gretchen had four children. Mary was their third child and only daughter. Mary's brothers were Joshua, Joseph, and Carl. Joseph grew up to become a soldier, and Joshua became a sailor.

1777–1778	1778	1822	1832
Spent the winter at Valley Forge.	*Fought at the Battle of Monmouth on June 28.*	*Began getting a **pension** from Pennsylvania.*	*Died on January 22 in Carlisle, Pennsylvania.*

Working on the Farm

Joshua and Joseph were adults by the time Mary was born. They both left the Ludwig farm to start their own families. Life on a farm was hard work. With the two oldest boys gone, the Ludwigs needed Mary to do a lot of the work that the boys used to do.

Besides helping Gretchen with housework, Mary helped her father take care of the cows. She milked the cows and carried pails of milk. She shoveled hay and worked in the fields to grow plants to feed the cows.

Farmers in Mary's time not only produced goods to sell to others. They also grew all the food their families needed to survive.

Mary and her family had to work hard to earn money.
This picture shows money and a wallet from the 1750s.

Mary's younger brother, Carl, got to go to school. When Mary was growing up, girls usually didn't go to school. Some parents thought it was a waste of time to send girls to school because girls usually didn't get jobs or make money for the family.

Mary grew to be a strong, young girl. She was a hard worker who made life on the farm a little easier for her parents. The Ludwigs were hard workers but they never had much money. Small farms didn't make people rich.

Moving Away

When Mary was thirteen years old, a woman named Anna Irvine visited friends near the Ludwig farm. Anna saw how much work Mary did every day, and she had an idea.

Anna and her husband, William, needed a girl about Mary's age to do work around their house in Carlisle, Pennsylvania. Anna asked Mrs. Ludwig if she could hire Mary. She would pay Mary for her work, and Mary could send the money back to the Ludwigs.

This house probably looks a lot like what the Irvines' house looked like. It was built about 1765 in Carlisle, Pennsylvania.

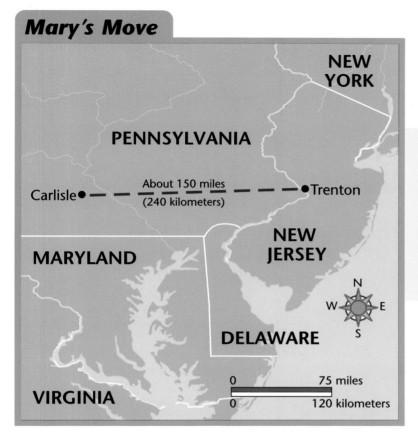

Mary's Move

About 150 miles (240 kilometers)

NEW YORK

PENNSYLVANIA

Carlisle — Trenton

MARYLAND

NEW JERSEY

DELAWARE

VIRGINIA

0   75 miles
0   120 kilometers

Mary moved from the farm near Trenton to Carlisle. Trenton became the capital of New Jersey in 1790.

It was a hard choice for Mr. and Mrs. Ludwig to make. They really needed the extra money that Mary would make, but she would live with the Irvines. Carlisle was about 150 miles (240 kilometers) away from the farm. They might never see Mary again.

Finally, they decided Mary could work for the Irvines. Living in Carlisle would be different than the farm. The work was still hard, but Carlisle was a busy town, not quiet and lonely like the farm.

Carlisle and Marriage

William Irvine was a doctor and an important man in the town of Carlisle. He later became a general in George Washington's army. Many people came to the Irvine house, which gave Mary the chance to meet people. One of the people she met was a young barber named William Hays.

William Hays

William's family came from Germany, like Mary's dad. When they came to America, their name was Heis. It was easier for the people living in Carlisle to say the name Hays, so they changed their name.

This is the earliest known drawing of Carlisle, Pennsylvania. It was drawn in about 1797.

William and Mary's Wedding

William and Mary were married at the Irvine home on July 24, 1769. Later, the house was torn down, and a church was built there.

William and Mary fell in love. They were married in 1769, which was not long after Mary went to work for the Irvines.

Now that Mary was married, she was very busy. She not only had to work at the Irvines' house but also had to cook and clean in her own home. Mary was just fourteen years old. As Mary's life was changing, so was life in the American **colonies.**

In addition to washing clothes, cleaning, and making meals, women in Mary's time also made soap and candles at home.

War Breaks Out

The American **colonies** were ruled by Great Britain. Laws were made in Great Britain, but the people in the colonies did not have a say in deciding what the laws would be. The colonists showed King George III of Great Britain that they were not happy about this situation. They refused to buy anything from Great Britain.

In 1774, men from all the colonies met. They formed the **Continental Congress.** The Second Continental Congress approved Thomas Jefferson's **Declaration of Independence** in 1776. It told Great Britain and the world why America should be its own country.

George Washington, shown here in 1772, was a leader in the Congress.

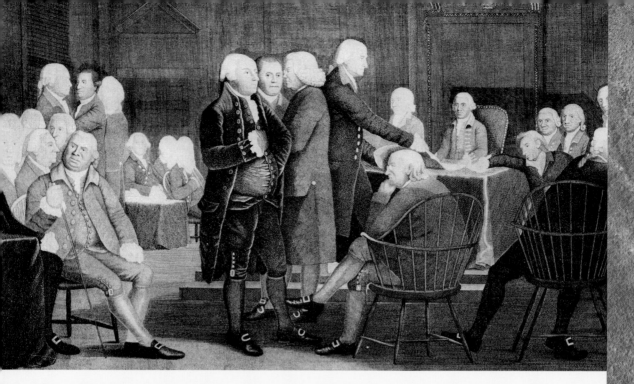

This painting shows members of the Continental Congress voting in Philadelphia, Pennsylvania. They adopted the Declaration of Independence on July 4, 1776.

The king wanted to keep the colonies. He sent soldiers to the colonies to make sure Great Britain's laws were obeyed. Battles broke out between the colonists and the British, and the **Revolutionary War** began.

William Hays joined the American army in 1776. It didn't take Mary long to decide that she would rather face danger with William than to be without him.

Women and the War

Life was not easy for the women who followed the soldiers of the **Revolutionary War.** The soldiers worked hard during the day training to be fighters, but the women worked even harder.

The women cooked meals, washed clothes, and took care of sick people and children. They worked hard because they wanted to be near the men they loved. They also wanted to help the new country of the United States become free.

Some women traveled with their husbands as they left to fight in the Revolutionary War.

A Different Road

Once when Washington's army marched into the city of Philadelphia, Pennsylvania, he made the women travel by a different road so they would not be seen.

When the battles began, the women went onto the battlefields to help. They carried water for the soldiers, and they cared for soldiers who had been hurt.

Mary was one of those hardworking women. General George Washington knew that the women following his army were needed if the United States was going to win the war. But historians say that he was **embarrassed** because his army needed their help.

In this painting, George Washington and his wife, Martha, are seen visiting sick and hurt soldiers.

Valley Forge

In the summer and fall of 1777, Washington and his men won a few battles against the British. Then, they began to lose battles. The **Continental Congress** did not give Washington as many supplies as he needed. He didn't have **shelter** for the soldiers and could not buy enough food or pay his soldiers.

This painting shows the American army marching to Valley Forge.

In the winter, Washington moved his army to a camp called Valley Forge in Pennsylvania. It was a long, cold winter for the Americans, but Washington's men trained hard. Mary and William were in Valley Forge for the entire winter.

A Soldier's Buttons

Soldiers in Mary's time sometimes used the brass and gold buttons on their uniforms as a type of money. They would trade their buttons for food or drinks.

At Valley Forge, there were not enough tents or houses for the soldiers to sleep in. Some had to sleep in the snow. There was not enough food for everyone to eat. Men and women didn't have enough warm clothes to wear. Some men and women didn't have a coat or shoes to wear.

Some people left the army and went home. The soldiers who stayed trained hard under General Friedrich Von Steuben. He taught them how to move on the battlefield. When spring came, Washington's army was tough and hungry for a victory.

To be fed and stay at Valley Forge, Mary had to sew, cook, clean, and do other work, like the soldiers shown in the background.

Battle of Monmouth

In 1778, government leaders in France said that France's army would help the United States fight the British. The British army marched from Pennsylvania toward New York to meet the French.

In June 1778, Washington caught up to the British army near Monmouth, New Jersey. On a hot day in June, the two armies fought each other for almost twelve hours. It became known as the Battle of Monmouth. The air was thick with the smoke from **cannons** and the cries of soldiers who had been shot. Coming back from a well carrying her water pitcher, Mary found an American soldier who had been shot.

The battle lasted from the early morning until about five o'clock.

William's job was to clean and get the cannon ready for the next shot. Mary took over for him after he collapsed.

She picked the soldier up and put him on her shoulders. She carried him to safety as bullets flew through the air around her. After she saved the man's life, she found her husband William lying near his cannon. The heat had made him **collapse.**

A soldier yelled for the men to move the cannon off the battlefield. Instead, Mary stepped forward. The woman who the American soldiers called Molly Pitcher loaded the cannon and fired it at the British army.

Sergeant Molly

Mary had spent many hours watching William fire the **cannon.** She knew just what to do. Mary bent over to pick up a cannonball to load into the cannon. She heard another cannonball scream through the air. It flew right through her legs and ripped her dress.

Mary was in danger not only from the guns of the British, but also from her husband's cannon. If the cannon became too hot from firing, it could explode and kill her. The water that Mary brought was also used to cool off the cannons.

These people in the state of Maryland recreated what a battle in the Revolutionary War was like.

This drawing of Molly at the Battle of Monmouth shows Washington and other generals in the background.

Mary kept firing the cannon until the battle was over. During the **Revolutionary War,** the winner of a battle was the army that held the most land or ground at the end of the day. The American army won the Battle of Monmouth. The Americans had won an important victory.

General Washington heard what Mary had done. He honored her by making her a **sergeant** in the army. From then on, Mary was known as "Sergeant Molly."

Molly's Last Years

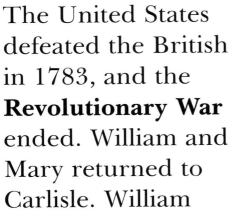

The United States defeated the British in 1783, and the **Revolutionary War** ended. William and Mary returned to Carlisle. William went back to being a barber, and Mary was a **servant** in another family's home. William died in 1789.

Since William and Mary never had any children, she was alone. A few years later, Mary married a man named John McCauly. In about 1807, John disappeared. Nobody is sure if he died or just left Carlisle.

Molly's Award

Today, several groups in the United States give Molly Pitcher awards to honor people who support U.S. soldiers.

This Molly Pitcher award is given by the United States Field Artillery Association.

Mary lived the rest of her life in Carlisle. Historians have said that the people who knew Mary remembered her as being the first person in town to help out a person in need.

In 1822, the state of Pennsylvania gave Mary a **pension.** The state gave Mary a yearly payment for the rest of her life for her heroic actions at the Battle of Monmouth. Mary died on January 22, 1832.

This photo shows Mary's grave and monument in Carlisle in 1955. She is shown holding an instrument called a ramrod.

The Other Molly Pitcher

Another woman in American history also had the nickname Molly Pitcher. Margaret Cochran Corbin was married to John Corbin. His job was to load a **cannon** for the American army in the **Revolutionary War.**

On November 16, 1776, British soldiers attacked **Fort** Washington in New York. John was helping another soldier fire a cannon at the British, but the **gunner** was killed. John fired the cannon, but then he was killed, too.

This picture of Margaret Cochran Corbin was drawn by the artist Herbert Knotel.

A Soldier's Wife

If a soldier was killed in the Revolutionary War, his wife could stay and help the other soldiers. But, in both the British and American armies, she had to get married to another soldier in no more than three days.

Margaret took John's place and began to fire the cannon. The British fired back with **grapeshot.** Grapeshot was a lot of smaller pieces of metal shot from a cannon instead of a **cannonball.** Margaret was hit in the arm, chest, and jaw. For the rest of her life, Margaret could never use her left arm again.

This plaque was placed near Margaret's grave in New York.

Remembering the Women of the War

The **Revolutionary War** might not have been won without the brave actions of women like Mary Hays McCauly and Margaret Cochran Corbin. Thousands of women helped the American army win the war. Most of the women didn't fire a **cannon** or a gun, but they were just as brave. American women were on the battlefields of the war carrying water and helping hurt soldiers.

Mary Hays McCauly lived in this house in Carlisle, Pennsylvania. The house was torn down in 1899.

In many ways, the women known as Molly Pitcher were the first female American soldiers. Today, thousands of women proudly serve in the American armed forces.

Women faced the same bullets and **cannonballs** the soldiers did when they tried to nurse the hurt soldiers on the battlefield. The women, who were wives of the American soldiers, also had to face cold, icy winters without shoes or warm coats.

Some men of the army became heroes in the war and we know their names, but many women helped them stay on the battlefields. Without the women of the Revolutionary War, the United States would not have the freedom it has today.

Glossary

cannon large gun from which large metal balls called cannonballs are shot

colony group of people who moved to another land but who are still ruled by the country they moved from. People who live in a colony are called colonists.

collapse to fall to the ground because of extreme tiredness

Continental Congress group of men that spoke and acted for the colonies that became the United States. It was formed to deal with complaints about Great Britain.

Declaration of Independence document that said the United States was an independent nation. Independent means not under the control or rule of another person or government.

embarrassed uncomfortable and shameful

fort building with strong walls and guns to defend against attacks from enemies

grapeshot cluster of small metal balls shot from a cannon

gunner person who fires a cannon

pension payment given to soldiers who no longer serve in the army

Revolutionary War war from 1775 to 1783 in which American colonists won freedom from Great Britain

sergeant soldier who gives orders to some soldiers, such as privates, but takes orders from other soldiers, such as officers

servant attendant or helper

shelter lodging or housing

More Books to Read

Burke, Rick. *Deborah Sampson*. Chicago: Heinemann Library, 2003.

Rockwell, Anne F. *They Called Her Molly Pitcher*. New York: Random House Children's Books, 2002.

Ruffin, Frances E. *Molly Pitcher*. New York: Rosen Publishing Group, 2002.

Places to Visit

Molly Pitcher's Grave
Old Graveyard & Two Cemeteries
Carlisle, Cumberland County, Pennsylvania

Monmouth Battlefield State Park
347 Freehold-Englishtown Road
Manalapan, New Jersey 07726
Visitor Information: (732) 462-9616

Valley Forge National Historical Park
North Gulph Road
Valley Forge, Pennsylvania 19482
Visitor Information: (610) 783-1077

Index